HOW
TO
BE
A
STAND-UP
COMIC

Richard Belzer,

Larry Charles

and

Rick Newman

Villard Books · New York · 1988

HOW
TO
BE
A
STAND-UP
COMIC

Library of Congress Cataloging-in-Publication Data

Belzer, Richard.
How to be a stand-up comic.

1. Stand-up comedy.   I. Charles, Larry.
II. Newman, Rick.   III. Title
PN1969.C65B44   1988   792.7′028   87-40575
ISBN 0-394-56239-9

Designed by Oksana Kushnir

9 8 7 6 5 4 3 2
First Edition

PREFACE

by Rick Newman

A little while back, I decided that what was needed in this world was a book called *How to Be a Stand-up Comic.* I felt that because I had started the comedy club Catch a Rising Star, managed many comedians, produced TV specials and seen thousands of stand-up comics, I knew something about comedy. After sixteen years in the business I'm sure of three things:

1. You can't teach funny—it's like teaching someone to be short.
2. I don't like comedians.
3. I *love* comedians.

I began to think: *Who'd be the best comedian to bring into this project?* There was only one, as far as I was concerned, so I turned to the Belz, who loved the idea. It turned out, in fact, that he too had been thinking of such a book.

Richard Belzer is the comic's comic. He exemplifies stand-up comedy for the eighties. He's smart, tough, controversial, observant and, above all, funny. We agreed that the book should be:

1. Funny
2. Educational
3. Real

One of the first things to learn in comedy, is that all performers need writers to write gags for them, to bounce jokes off of, and generally to abuse, so we decided that Larry Charles should help write this book. Larry writes funny, bounces well, and takes abuse wonderfully. He also loved the idea.

Comics say there is no greater exhilaration than to stand on stage and make people laugh. I doubt there is any worse feeling than bombing in front of an audience. Comedy is the bravest thing in the world. If you're an actor, you're part of a cast. A singer is part of a band—and an audience is trained to applaud after every song. But with stand-up, if an audience doesn't like your material, they don't like *you,* plain and simple. A comedian lives or dies by how funny his or her last line was.

Comedy is "hot" now. This shouldn't be a surprise. Times are hard, and people want to laugh. What is a surprise is the extent to which comedians have become cultural heroes. Comics like Lenny Bruce, Woody Allen, Robin Williams and Lily Tomlin have changed the way we think. Shows like *Saturday Night Live* and *Late Night with David Letterman* have changed our attitudes.

Why have we written this book? Money. No, seriously—because we love comedy and because there can never be enough comedians. Even when we go for the lowest of the low gags, we know you'll still learn something: how to use a mike, how to write some simple material, and how to deliver that material. You'll learn how hard it is to be funny or, at least, how hard it is to be funny *and* earn a living at it!

It's been said that comedy sometimes stems from anger, but we think it's better to channel anger into comedy than to take an ice-pick to Aunt Millie. In fact, think about it like this: Forget about the money . . . if everyone bought a copy of this book, there might not be any more wars.

There is a great Preston Sturges movie called *Sullivan's Travels*. It's about a successful Hollywood film director who's tired of making popular comedies because he thinks they're unimportant. Sullivan sets out to learn about the world so he can make an "important" tragedy. Tragedy winds up striking his own life; he ends up on a chain gang, nearly a broken man. One day the prisoners are allowed to watch a movie, a silly cartoon. Sullivan sees this group of sad men laugh and realizes, for the first time, that the ability to make people laugh is a great and wonderful gift. It still is!

CONTENTS

It's a funny world we live in . . .

. . . filled with the crazy absurdities
of everyday life . . .

It doesn't take a genius
to see how funny life can be.

> RICHARD'S
> I.Q.
> TEST SCORE: 57

And with that in mind, I, Richard Belzer, aka the Belz, *your* Belz, ladies and gentlemen, your *personal* Belz, can turn anyone—*anyone*—into a stand-up comedian.

Well, *almost* anyone.

Hey, wait a minute. I've got an idea. We'll choose *you*. Yes, *you,* you little sucker. You bought the book already, so why not? I'll be sort of the Fagin of comedy. I'll lead you, show you the ropes, I'll . . . *Hey!* Don't close the . . . Don't close the cover! HEY! WAIT!

I can't breathe with the cover closed! **HELP!**

chapter

THE HISTORY OF
STAND-UP COMEDY

TIME LINE

4 million B.C.
First laugh:
God sees Adam naked
for the first time

12,500 B.C.
First punch line is
spoken: "Club my
wife . . . please!"

2500 B.C.
First monologue:
Moses burning bush
bit

A.D. 31
First catchphrase:
"Father, forgive them;
for they know not
what they do."

1932
Will Rogers dies in
plane crash

1938
Nipsey Russell is born

1968
Nixon is elected

1972
Hello, Larry premieres

1974
Marty Allen plays a
comic with a deadly
disease on *Medical
Center*

1988
This book

The Prehistoric Comic

"Ergghhh. Arrgghhh."

The Aztec Comic

"How many Mayans does it take to build a pyramid?"

The Israelite Comic

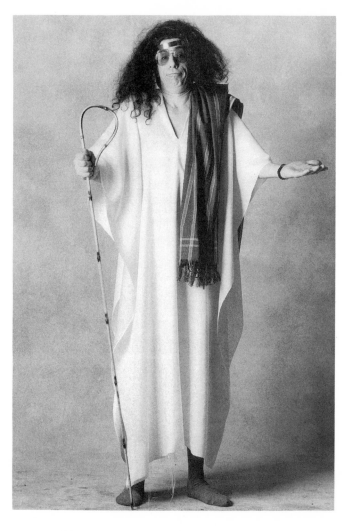

"And Noah said, 'Sorry, no pets.'"

The Dark Ages Comic

"Is that the plague or are you just glad to see me?"

The Renaissance Comic

"Yeah, *right*. And *I'm*
Leonardo da Vinci."

The New World Comic

"Twenty-four dollars is a little *steep* for Manhattan, don't you think, Featherhead?"

The Civil War Comic

"And so Lincoln says, 'I need a war like
I need a hole in the head.'"

The Modern Comic

"The Belz, babe."

This chapter is directed to kids and
their parents. 'Cause you know,
mom and dad, the kids are the future.
And if we don't all get along,
well, brother and sister . . .

EARLY-WARNING SIGNS OF THE STAND-UP PERSONALITY

These are the early-warning signs of the stand-up personality:

Do you think the death of a
relative is funny?

Do you enjoy doing impressions of handicapped people?

Do you mercilessly ridicule nerdy classmates?

"Nice tie, Waldo."

Do you make tough guys and bullies
laugh to avoid getting your ass kicked?

"Don't hit me.
I'll beat myself up."

If you answered yes to any or all of these questions, then you may be suffering from an insidious syndrome known as Stand-up Personality Disorder. But you're not the only one. Millions, billions, perhaps even trillions suffer from this dreaded condition. So, please, read on; help is on the way. In the back of this book are phone numbers of comedy clubs in your area, where trained professionals are prepared to respond rudely but promptly to your situation. Give them a call day or night, and, oh, by the way, do me a favor: Don't mention my name. . . . If anyone asks you, you don't know me. Okay, Sparky? I knew you'd understand. Just tell 'em Leno or Garry Shandling told you to call. Those guys make more money than I do. . . . Thanks.

NEWMAN'S NOTE

Timing is everything—in comedy and in life!

NEWMAN'S NOTE

Attitude is crucial. A lot of bitter, angry performers think that anger automatically translates into comedy. Not true.

In some ways, comedy seems to be getting less angry. Think of Robin Williams, Billy Crystal and Steve Martin. They're wild, at times they put the audience down, but they're not *angry* up on stage. Attitude is crucial.

Belz's Anatomy:
A GRAPHIC DEPICTION OF THE NEUROLOGICAL WORKINGS OF THE COMEDY BRAIN

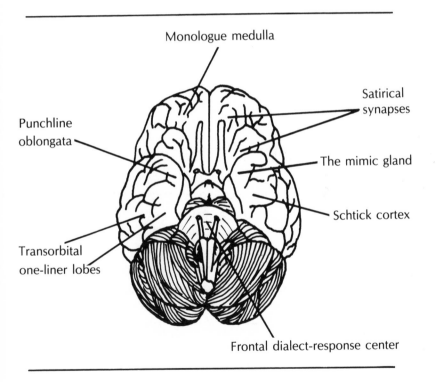

Monologue medulla

Satirical synapses

Punchline oblongata

The mimic gland

Schtick cortex

Transorbital one-liner lobes

Frontal dialect-response center

First of all, you must make a commitment to a comedy career. It can't be a casual thing. You can't be a part-time comedian any more than you can be a part-time brain surgeon. It's a life decision, and you have to dedicate yourself to it every day. Oh, you can have a day job and go work out at the clubs at night, but *never* forget that the whole idea is eventually to become a

A COMEDIAN PREPARES

full-time comedian. You're never going to make it as a stand-up comic if, in the back of your mind, you're thinking that you can always wind up being an accountant.

The best advice I can give you is to go on as much as you can, every night, in any situation where there's an audience—doing jokes to a mirror or on a typewriter is not a real barometer of how funny you are as a performer. You may think that your jokes are funny, your friends may think you're funny, but trust me: It's not until you can make a room full of strangers laugh that you can feel you're on the right track.

One thing to keep in mind always: Failure is inevitable in early stand-up comedy. No matter how naturally funny you are, if you don't have a professional structure to your act and the proper frame for your material, even the funniest things won't get laughs. Without the right timing and the right presentation, you'll bomb. But remember: Everyone bombs in the beginning. That's why you have to be prepared to go on every night, if you can, in your local showcase clubs. Do whatever they allow—five, ten, fifteen minutes. Practice your routine, your delivery, your onstage persona.

The earlier you are in your career, the less material you have, so tape your act every night to hear where the laughs are coming from. Listen to when you're rushing the material. Listen to when you're too slow. One of the biggest mistakes that beginning comedians make—in fact, even experienced comedians make—is rushing when they don't hear laughs. Take your time—unless you're noted for talking fast, which is a different discussion.

Prepare to fail. Say it out loud: *Prepare to fail*—night after night in some cases and for long periods of time. I've seen people who were real bad for a *real* long time who persisted and kept going on and eventually got better. There's no other way to do it. Fail, practice, fail. Keep going on—and on.

You should also watch *The Tonight Show Starring Johnny Carson* and *Late Night with David Letterman*. Watch the comics and learn from what they do. But don't watch a comedian come on and do his or her five minutes and think to yourself, "Oh, that looks easy." It takes a lot of work, many years of work in many cases, to distill material into that five minutes, that special, slick five minutes on *The Tonight Show*.

Usually, the easier it looks, the harder it is. People *acquire* that ease and grace—it's a craft. The blacksmith can't make the horseshoe the first time out; he's got to apprentice and learn and pay the dues. A lot of the older comics talk about the early days of vaudeville, doing five hundred shows a year. Some of those guys did five shows a day, working afternoons and nights to refine their twelve minutes—and because there wasn't TV, they were able to do the same act, that same twelve minutes, for twenty years. Now there's more of a demand for new material, although there are still a lot of places to go out and work. There are several hundred nightclubs where people can work on their material [see Appendix II], but it's like in sports—even the farm system has gotten more sophisticated.

You should plan a career in stages, not just say, "I'm going to do five minutes on *The Tonight Show* and then get my own TV series." There are levels of clubs as well as levels of acts. You could be an opening act for a couple of years, then a middle act and then a headliner. There are comics who work the club circuit you've probably never heard of, but they make a very good living. They may never be on television, but they have skill and talent, and they love what they do. Really wanting to be a stand-up comedian is more than wanting to be a star. You might want both, but if you love being a stand-up comedian, the idea of getting paid for doing comedy rather than working in a factory should be it's own reward. You have to set realistic goals for yourself; an immediate three-picture deal is *not* a realistic goal.

It took me two or three years before I made what I would call a decent living as a comedian, and I had *two* jobs at that time. I was in *The National Lampoon Show* off-Broadway, and I was emceeing at the New York comedy club Catch a Rising Star. It takes a long time. There are some people who should be bigger stars than they are, and there are some who don't deserve to be as big as they are, but there's one thing you have to realize—there's no logic to this business. I like to think that talent does win out eventually, but it doesn't always happen in storybook fashion or as fast as we would like it to. There are no rules as to why somebody makes it and somebody else doesn't, but there *are* formulas and patterns from which to learn.

In the seventies, there was what I call the Gabe/Jimmy/Freddy syndrome. Gabe Kaplan, Jimmy Walker and Freddy Prinze each did the same thing: worked out for a few years in showcase clubs, got on *The Tonight Show,* and then got a TV series. For a while that was what everyone aspired to.

Gabe Kaplan is an interesting case. He was working out in the Catskill Mountains and in the small clubs around New York (of which there were very few then). He was of the Jewish-Catskill genre of comedian, which is not meant to be demeaning—it's a legitimate comedy tradition. Then he went on *The Tonight Show* with a bit that he had been doing for a couple of years—a version of *The Dating Game* with old people—and he *killed* the audience. He got huge laughs with the famous line: "The average age in Miami is deceased." Well, that's not his joke—it's an *old* joke—but it *became* his. He was brought back to *The Tonight Show* a few times, got more and more popular, and developed a routine based on ranking out his friends at school.

That routine instigated the series *Welcome Back, Kotter.* And there you have it—success.

Freddy Prinze, who came from Spanish Harlem, was working small clubs, doing Richard Pryor and Redd Foxx routines, until somebody told him to start doing original material. Eventually he started doing his own stuff and got kind of hot. He did a shot on *ABC Late Night* with Jack Paar in 1973. Freddy's manager at the time, Dave Jonas, sent a tape of the Paar performance to *The Tonight Show.* They loved it and put him on the following week. The night he was on, Sammy Davis, Jr., was on the show, and before Freddy came out, Sammy sang and danced and did a great set, which got the audience extremely excited. Then Freddy came out and Sammy got up from the couch and ran around the back of the camera to watch Freddy. The audience saw that and picked up on it, and Freddy did great. So it was a magic night—everything fell together at the right time. That's something you cannot predict. There are comics who have been on *The Tonight Show* forty times, and they're *funny*—but you can't remember one line they did. Freddy had a memorable catchphrase—"It's not my job"—and it caught on.

Jimmy Walker was working in Harlem when David Brenner saw him and said he had to come downtown to perform at The Improvisation, another New York club. Jimmy was wearing a dashiki and doing local material, but he came downtown, started working those audiences, and started doing well. He also had a catchphrase—"Dyn-o-mite!" And he also got a TV series that was, more or less, based on his stage persona.

The one thing those three guys have in common—for better or for worse—is they each had material and a style that an audience could identify with easily.

People identify with someone for different reasons: appearance, style, likability. Despite their ethnic origins and their urban backgrounds, Gabe, Jimmy and Freddy had material that was universal. The problems they dealt with, as well as the characters and personalities they discussed, were recognizable and could have been from any ethnic group. The themes that pervaded their comedy were also universal.

Before the Gabe/Jimmy/Freddy

syndrome, there were George Carlin, David Steinberg and Robert Klein, the top comics of the late sixties and a link to the Mort Sahl/Bob Newhart/Shelley Berman era of stand-up comedy. Those comics exhibited an intelligence that hadn't been seen before in stand-up comedy. They educated as well as made people laugh.

Timing was crucial to their success, also. When they came along, the audience for comedy was younger and more literate. Their comedy reflected what was happening in other places in society—Kerouac, jazz, abstract painting. Comedians like Sahl and Newhart and Berman prepared by absorbing and reflecting the world around them, whether it was *Sputnik* or Madison Avenue or the Beat generation, the same way George Carlin and Robert Klein and David Steinberg reflected the Vietnam War and the irreverence of the sixties. In the sixties, for the first time, Americans were suspecting the government of lying and were disagreeing with institutions on issues like birth control. So comedians made fun of things that had been strictly taboo until then. In the seventies, a transitional decade between Vietnam and Reagan, Americans learned to accept a diversity in culture. Comedians like Jimmy, Freddy and Gabe learned to sanitize and homogenize that diversity and make it palpable to the masses. A comedian's preparation is keeping your eyes open to the world around you and turning your observations into humor, into a coherent routine.

A new trend is to go for an inane frivolity and mindless humor. Does this reflect the Reagan years? In a sense, yes. Part of preparation includes an awareness of what your audience wants and what they can take, an awareness of their sensibilities.

Fear is also a part of a comic's preparation. There's a lot of fear in performing and a lot of insecurity. A lot of this fear comes from the fact that stand-up comedy, like jazz improvisation, erupts from a mysterious source even the performer isn't familiar with. You don't know if you can do it every time you go out there and perform. Fear can be a negative thing, sending insecure comedians in search of artificial reinforcement (see a couple of things I like to call cocaine and heavy drinking), but a good comic can also turn it into an asset and use it to get an "edge"—a totally unique point of view that only the comic's own obsessions and fears can express. Fear can make a comedian vulnerable—and vulnerability has value.

Every comic has to deal differently with the fear of performing. Sometimes I need to be completely alone and silent before I go on. Lately, I find that I like talking to people and fooling around before a performance. Some comedians like to look at a stage performance as an extension of their offstage life. Others look at it as completely separate, so that when they go onstage, they transform themselves and do things they would never do in "real life."

Everyone prepares in a different way. What you've got to do now is settle into a pattern you find comfortable. Everything you've read here is valid—but now you've got to discover what works for you.

NEWMAN'S NOTE

A comic must use comedy clubs the way an athlete uses a gymnasium.

NEWMAN'S NOTE

To have a funny delivery, you should find something about *yourself* that's funny and develop that particular trait or characteristic.

Remember: Style comes from within.

HOW TO TELL A JOKE: THE BELZER METHOD

I thought, rather than simply talk about material and delivery, I'd illustrate, by taking a routine of mine that encompasses many of the points I want to make and breaking it down. Dissect it. So, if this book is the laboratory, then this routine—probably my most famous routine, about a rather unpleasant experience I had with Hulk Hogan and Mr. T—is the frog.

Enjoy it. Feel free to practice it. Learn from it.

And if I hear any of it on stage, I'll see you in court.

"Well, I've been working out lately, as you can tell. I'm lifting weights. I'm going to kick Hulk Hogan's ass when I see him. Hulk Hogan, my idol—I love Hulk Hogan.

"People still ask me if that incident was real. For those of you who don't know, I used to have a talk show called *Hot Properties.* And I had Hulk Hogan and Mr. T on my show, and Hulk Hogan tried to fuckin' kill me. This is a true story. I was in my dressing room and somebody from my staff—I shouldn't say, 'my staff,'—somebody who worked for me that I could fire came up to me and said, 'Mr. Belzer, ah, Mr. Belzer, ah, Richard, ah—we're going to get Hulk Hogan and Mr. T on the show.'

"I said, 'Yeah, sure.' And they said, 'No, no—they'll be good for the ratings.' I said, 'Ratings? Yeah, sure. I'll do anything for ratings.' You know, ratings are important.

"So I get a call a few minutes later from this woman who works for Hulk Hogan and Mr. T, and she says, 'Mr. T will not do this show unless there are fifty kids in the audience.' So I said, 'All right, all right.' So I hang up, and I say, 'What am I gonna do?' This is the day of the show, so I told these people who

[handwritten margin annotations: "Self-deprecation", "Sarcasm", "Set up information", "unexpected expletive", "character voice", "Inflated self-image", "Commercial vs. artistic considerations"]

work for me, I said, 'Look, go to some school. When the kids come out, sedate 'em, put *Hot Properties* T-shirts on 'em, throw 'em on a bus, bring 'em to the studio.

"Somehow we pulled it off. We got these kids from some school, I don't know—Our Lady of the Connecticut Turnpike School. So we got the kids, and then forty-five minutes before the show—I'm in makeup, as we say in our wacky industry—and I'm being made up. Somebody's making me up—I didn't exist then—and I'm being made up. And this woman who works for Mr. T comes into the makeup room and says, 'Uhh, Mr. Belzer, we're kind of walking on eggshells around Mr. T today because he's in a bad mood.'

"He's in a bad mood—Ethiopia's in a bad mood, you know what I'm saying? If this guy wasn't on *The A-Team,* he'd be doing thirty years for manslaughter—he's in a bad fuckin' mood? Gimme a break, will ya? To myself I said that. To myself. Out loud I said, 'Oh well, we'll take every precaution. We'll be very nice.'

"So then, about twenty minutes later, Mr. T does in fact show up, and this guy is the most intimidating, the

[handwritten margin notes: "vivid imagery"; "TENSION mounting"; "Funny name twist"; "Throw-away quick pun"; "aggressively saying what everybody feels"; "Interior monologue copping to reality"; "what we say vs. what we think"]

scariest person I've ever seen—he was like a fire hydrant from Mars. He had a baton with a spring in the middle that he was pumping. You know, the mohawk, and the diamonds and the chains around his neck and junk [imitating Mr. T grunting]. What genetic experiment went awry?

"'How you doin', Mr. T? It's nice to see you. We got the kids in the audience [more Mr. T imitations, grunting]. Finally I figured out through his interpreters, he was saying, 'Where's my dressing room? Where's my dressing room?' So I said, 'It's back there, babe.' He goes—he disappears back to the dressing room pumpin' this thing, you know.

"And about ten minutes later, Hulk Hogan shows up. Now Hulk Hogan is six-foot seven, he weighs 338 pounds. I'm six foot one, 150 pounds. *Newsweek* magazine called me the 'pencil-armed comedian.' Thank you, *Newsweek*. I'll be subscribing to you next week.

Hulk Hogan walks in and he's got the weirdest walk—like he just got fucked in the ass by a rhino. It's a real normal way for a man to walk. It's the Hulk/Rambo/Schwarzenegger walk, you know. These guys are so obsessed with

[handwritten annotations in margins: "Comedy simile", "imitation", "Setup", "payoff", "set up strong contrast", "Empathetic sarcasm", "Popular reference point"]

not being wimpy that they've perverted the whole idea of what it is to be a man.

"Hulk Hogan comes over to me. 'How ya doin', dude. What's happenin', dude. How are you, dude?' Dude? What am I, on a horse with a hat on in Colorado? Dude, my ass, babe. To myself I said that. Out loud I said, 'Oh, it's nice to see ya, Hulk. Glad you could do the show.' He said, 'Oh, you're a real funny dude. I'd like to be in your next movie, dude.' Yeah, like I own a fuckin' studio, and I can book him in a second. Again, to myself, I said that. He said, 'Where's my man, Mr. T?' I said, 'Well, he's back there doin' this [imitating Mr. T] you know.' So Hulk Hogan disappears back to Mr. T's dressing room.

"Then I have to start the show. I have to begin the show now, so I come out. I billboard the show—'Ladies and gentlemen, welcome to *Hot Properties*. We got fifty sedated kids in the audience. We got these two repressed fascist guys in the back who hate men and women. They'll be out in a second.'

"So the first guest out of the box is Mr. T. He comes out, and he still has the baton with the spring, you know, and on camera now, he's pumping this thing. He comes out, sits down next to me and just

[handwritten left margin: imitation]

[handwritten right margin: Interior monologue]

[handwritten right margin: Reality]

[handwritten left margin: ultimate no-holds-barred truth]

[handwritten right margin: Physical illustration (image of Mr. T sitting in dressing room)]

[handwritten right margin: Release of hearing taboo material in normally highly controlled environment]

[handwritten left margin: Reset the image]

■ 39

gives me one-word answers, grunts and groans. He's like the worst—he's a sexist, he's a racist, he's everything you don't want a person to be, you know. <u>And I, like an asshole, try to interview him,</u> 'cause it's a talk show . . .

Innocent attitude

"And I'm thinking to myself, while I'm interviewing him, <u>'Well, maybe there's a reason that he's like this.</u> Maybe there's a story, maybe there's an explanation that he's this way.' <u>No! He's a fuckin' asshole, ladies and gentlemen!</u> Some people are just assholes. Some people have a legitimate story—this guy is a fuckin' asshole.

Set up

Payoff

"And he says, 'All men in New York are wimps. All men in New York—' All men in New York are wimps! And I said, 'Why do you say that?' 'While I was on the subway today, I beat up three muggers.' <u>Right, right, sure, right. To myself, I said that.</u> Out loud I said, 'Oh, I'm glad you're cleaning up the subways, because—' <u>Then I made the mistake of using a word he didn't know. I said the word *exclaim,* and he got really pissed off at me and said, 'I don't know that word. I'm from the street.'</u>

Challenge mr. T

Copping to own cowardice

Build tension

"And I said, 'Well, I'm from the street, too, and I <u>learned</u> the word, okay, babe?' That I said out loud, and the

Incredible true life act of bravery

audience went, 'Whoooo.' And he started pumping that baton more. Smoke started coming out of his hair. He started remembering Louis Farrakhan speeches, you know. It got real scary. So I go to commercial, a Pepsi commercial. That's a great thing you can do on a talk show, you can go to commercial. It'd be great if you could do that in real life, you know, a sticky situation: 'We'll be right back after this—' You can't do that in real life, only on a talk show.

"Now, during the commercial, I lean over to Mr. T, and I said, 'Mr. T, babe, relax.' And he goes, 'I'm in character. I'm in character.' He's in character!! Take me to Uta Hagen fuckin' prison right now! He's in character. He's a method actor! You mean you chose to be this bully fuckin' punk, obnoxious asshole jerk?! To myself, I said that. Out loud I said, 'Oh, I should have known, I feel so stupid.'

"So we come back from commercial and Hulk Hogan comes out with fresh horn marks on his ass. Got rhino burns on his cheeks now. He comes out, sits down next to me and says, 'I've been watching you backstage—you know, I told my man, Mr. T, not to hurt anybody, and you probably heard about that—and that's why you're giving him a *stream of consciousness* hard time, and de-dit, de-de-dit, ——— de-de-dittle-dittle . . ." He starts singing scat on my show—at least that's what it sounded like.

"So I'm thinking I've got to control the situation, so I say, 'Let's have a little demonstration.' I figured maybe we'll fool around a little bit. Little did I know *Tone change from frivolous to serious* he was going to try to <u>fuckin' kill me.</u> I mean, Johnny Carson has a show, Letterman has a show and eight hundred other people have shows—none of them ever almost got fuckin' killed on the show. So this wasn't anywhere in my mind at all. We go over to the demonstration area, and on the way over there, Hulk Hogan leans over to Mr. T and says—I didn't hear this until they played it back for me later—but at the time he said to Mr. T, 'I'm gonna make him squeal.' Now if I'd heard that, I would have been <u>Ralph Kramden for a</u> *Reference point for fear* <u>month, 'Homina, homina, homina, homina . . .'</u> But I didn't hear it, so I go over to the demonstration area where we *Contrast for what's to come* <u>cook soufflés and B. B. King plays</u>—it's an innocuous area.

"You know, it's show business: I'm a talk-show host, you know, I'm really happy, I got my own show, and this fucking guy—he gives a front-chin lock. You know, some people call it the sleeper hold. Technically it's the front-chin lock. My head here—if you had a picture with a caption on it—Belzer's head here. His arms are as big as mine are gonna be if I pump iron for eight hundred fuckin' years. A real normal thing to do.

Hyperbole

"So he gets me in a front-chin lock and he starts squeezing—I figured he's foolin' around. And then he squeezes more, and it starts hurting—and holy shit, my brain goes, "Check please! No oxygen, I'm outta here, babe, right? Thank you." So he knocks me out.

Anthropomorphic Reference: inanimate object infused with personality

"Now he didn't become a wrestler because he quit Harvard, okay? He knocks me out in his arms, I'm unconscious, and what does he do? He lets me go. Okay? I fall down—I'm unconscious already—I fall down to the ground, and I hit the back of my head on the floor of the studio, split my head open. For some reason, I jumped up and said, 'We'll be right back.' I don't know how I did that. I actually did that in shock, I did that. Talk about show business in your blood—it was coming out of my fuckin' head. The whole industry was floating on the back of my head.

"So I went backstage. They put me in an ambulance. I went to the hospital that night. I got eight stitches in my head. I'm in bed that night in the hospital, and I'm watching TV, and I think, maybe it'll be on the news. Maybe it'll be on the fuckin' news.

"Every station had it on that night. Channel 2: Richard Belzer, Hulk Hogan—BOOM! Channel 4: 'Was it fake, was it real?'—BOOM! 'Judge for yourself, let's see it in slow motion'—BOOM! 'Let's speed it up'—BOOM! 'Let's run it back, see it again'—BOOM, BOOM!

Easy to relate to aftermath

"I got ten more stitches watching the fuckin' thing. Jesus Christ. And that night I had a nightmare in the hospital. I had a nightmare that my first show back would go something like this—this is after this ugly incident, I come back to the first show at *Hot Properties:* [Distorted voice—à la brain damage] 'Thank oo vay much, lays an' genmen. Is goo be back on da show.'

Fantasy projection

"To *myself* I said that—well, that's the story of that. It's a hell of a way to get material."

NEWMAN'S NOTE

Working as a sketch comedian (à la Second City, The Groundlings, etc.) is great practice for being a stand-up comic. It's great comedy training.

NEWMAN'S NOTE

Everyone's waiting for the next great comedy team.

If you decide to work as a team, remember: Your stage persona must work as a *whole*, not just as two individuals. Your timing must work with a partner as well as the audience.

One good thing about working with a partner: You're not up on stage sweating it out all by yourself.

NEWMAN'S NOTE

Everyone bombs—that horrible feeling when all you hear is that complete, dead silence. You'll break into a sweat and shake all over. If you're *lucky enough not to pass out,* just take a deep breath and keep going. It's all you can do.

A comedian's timing must feel natural. That feeling can only come by performing. Practice, practice, practice—in front of an audience!

A good manager usually charges between 15 percent and 20 percent of a performer's earnings. If you're being charged more than 20 percent, you're being ripped off. If you're being charged less than 15 percent, chances are that you don't have top-of-the-line management.

At the beginning, it's not important what you're being paid as long as you're getting the work. If you don't have a manager, check around with other comedians as to what seems like fair payment for the work you do, or use your own judgment.

Sometimes an audience doesn't laugh out loud—but they're still a good audience. This lack of feedback is confusing and not very gratifying—but just play through it and don't lose your composure.

Try to put together a three-minute routine.

Make sure it has a beginning, a middle and an end. Jokes must be linked together as best as you can. *Segue* is a crucial comedy word.

Obviously, having an audience is crucial, but you've got to start somewhere. Practice your routine over and over again into a tape recorder. Listen to it over and over again!

Use a mirror, if you are comfortable with this; some people don't like to look at themselves.

When you're ready, perform for a group of friends who have a discerning, critical sense of humor.

Remember: People who laugh at anything *won't do you any good!*

There have been many great thinkers,
theorists and philosophers in the annals
of stand-up. Many have publicly
commented on the metaphysical nature
of stand-up comedy. Herewith are
some of their thoughts:

"If it's funny, it's funny."
—Red Buttons
"Timing is everything."
—Arthur Schopenhauer
"Don't work dirty."
—Milton Berle
"Pick your spots."
—Immanuel Kant
"Have a gimmick."
—Pat Cooper
"Props are the enemies of wit."
—Bertrand Russell

THE ETHICS, MORALITY AND PHILOSOPHY OF STAND-UP

All right now, we're going to try to cover the ethics, morality and philosophy of stand-up comedy, without being too solemn.

First of all, the number one rule of all stand-up comedy is "Thou shalt not steal." The one major taboo of stand-up comedy is taking another comedian's material and doing it verbatim, or changing the setup but using the same punch line, or altering the body of the joke but using the same material. There are people who are famous within the business for stealing. And then there is someone like Milton Berle who made a career out of stealing—he literally did steal everybody else's material—but he became a megastar. So there are two comedy commandments: "Thou shalt not steal," but "If thou dost, thou *shalt* kill the audience."

As far as comedy ethics go, there are comedians who have the capacity to talk about things that wouldn't normally be talked about in stand-up comedy. For instance, Lenny Bruce talked about Hitler and the Holocaust and Truman and the bomb and all that stuff. He did a routine about Bobby Frank, the little kid who was murdered by Leopold and Loeb. He was able to do it because he found a satirical point of view about these things—a way of looking at the death of Bobby Frank and Hitler that articulated thoughts that people in the audience could recognize but could never have verbalized themselves. He made sense in a way that was to some shocking, to some a revelation, to others offensive.

Are there still taboo topics? Well, Sam Kennison does a routine where he lies face down on the stage and talks about this guy who's lived his life and now he's dead

50 ▪

and he's on the table, and a gay mortician starts fucking him in the ass. It's one of the funniest things I have ever seen, and it has a point. Sam calls it "the ultimate insult of life." But if you describe this routine, it sounds tasteless. Anal intercourse, death, homosexuality, necrophilia—just when you thought it was safe to go back into the nightclub, Kennison comes up with a new taboo.

There's another genre: jokes that emerge from tragedies. The day after the *Challenger* exploded, while pieces of it were still falling into the sea, comics were doing jokes about it. That's how fast jokes happen. But where do those jokes come from? There's a collective unconscious reflex—as soon as you hear about something that's tragic or that hints at mortality or grotesqueness, you automatically make a joke about it. You laugh to try to dilute it. It makes sense: We all make jokes about the things we fear most, and comedians make jokes for a living, so therefore the "sick" jokes will come out of the comic community first. I think there's a therapeutic value to it, a cathartic defense mechanism that helps us survive.

"What was the last thing Christa McAuliffe said?" *" 'What's this button for . . .' "*

"Rock Hudson had no friends, but he had neighbors *up the ass."*

The question is, are these jokes funny? Yes, they are. Do they somehow address a concern, a primal concern that we have? Yes, they do. They deal with things that are almost incomprehensible. They're ways of controlling the uncontrollable.

Are there things you *can't* talk about onstage? If you're a true comedian, you will have to find what you can live with and what will be acceptable to your audience. There's one joke I do that I'm on the fence about—about AIDS. I say, "Whoever would have thought that getting it in the ass five hundred times a day would be bad for you?" It's horrifying, it's offensive, but it's perceptive, and everybody responds to it—a perfect example of a sick joke.

It's a funny joke. It's also an important joke. Yet I'm ambivalent about telling it. That's an honest response. That's the best we can hope for in comedy: honesty.

Blue material: It's easier to get laughs when you say the word *fuck,* but I never recommend blue material for a comedian.

Of course, there are comics whose personas depend on blue material. The great ones in this category are: the Belz, of course; Richard Pryor; and Eddie Murphy. There's also a new, young "blue" comic named Rick Dukerman who's worth keeping an eye on.

In the old days, blue material couldn't be used on TV. Now, of course, with the advent of comedy on cable shows, that's different. But I still wouldn't be dependent on blue material. You'll be better off for it in the long run.

Stage presence: This can be defined as your visual persona—and it's the single most important element of your stage personality.

All successful comics have their own particular stage presence and style.

Your look is a matter of personal style.
In general, dress for comfort, but here
are a few helpful hints as you look
through your comedy closet.

The 1950s jazz-bop-heroin-addict-found-
dead-naked-in-a-bathroom look

The Alan King I-make-more-money-than-
you-I-live-in-a-big-house-in-Long-Island-or-
Beverly-Hills-I-can-make-fun-of-my-
mother-in-law-and-my-wife's-cooking-as-
long-as-I-make-four-million-a-year look

The I-should-have-been-a-teacher look

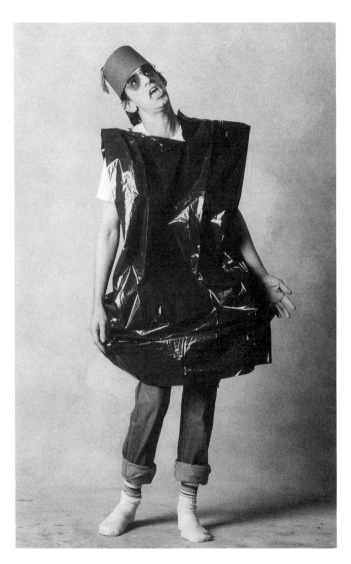

The my-look-is-my-act look

The let's-pretend-I'm-sitting-in-your-
living-room-even-though-I'd-never-hang-
out-with-you-in-real-life look

The Belz, babe.

THE MICROPHONE, YOUR FRIEND

Every little detail must be perfect up on stage if you expect to get laughs from your audience. Nothing can be overlooked. The microphone, for instance. There's a right and a wrong way to deal with "mike."

TRIED AND TRUE
STAGECRAFT

Mike Twirling

Right method

Wrong method

Mike Adjustment

Right method

Wrong method

Pacing

Right method

NEWMAN'S NOTE

Too many performers are tentative and
afraid around a microphone.

Remember: A microphone is not a
stiletto. Mikes don't kill—comedians
do.

Wrong method

HOW TO HANDLE
A HECKLER

Get the audience on your side.

Find their weakness.

Don't cry or run off stage. If they get the best of you, take it gracefully.

If you can get away with it, seek
revenge.

BELZER'S FIVE GUARANTEED-NEVER-TO-FAIL RESPONSES TO HECKLERS:

1. "If I want any more shit from you, I'll squeeze your head."
2. "This is what happens when a fetus doesn't get enough oxygen, ladies and gentlemen."
3. "Sir, I have a mike, you have a beer, God has a plan—and you're not in it."
4. "What do you use for birth control—your personality?"

   and when all else fails:

5. "Fuck you *and* your mother!"

The comedian is the wandering minstrel
of laughs, bringing mirth and mayhem
to people of all geographical and
economic realities. The road is the
comic's heaven and hell, his purgatory,
his limbo, his paradise, his home.

THE ROAD

■ 79

Here is how one comic sees this
great, complex, majestic land of ours:

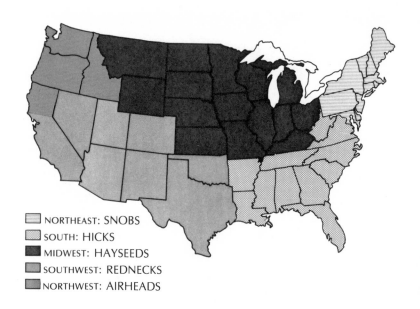

☐ NORTHEAST: SNOBS
☐ SOUTH: HICKS
■ MIDWEST: HAYSEEDS
☐ SOUTHWEST: REDNECKS
▓ NORTHWEST: AIRHEADS

Let's examine how the road works.

Booking: You can't just head out on the highway and expect to make the big bucks. No, you need someone to call ahead, make arrangements, take care of the working and living conditions. This someone is called an "agent," a "representative" or a "booker," and you should learn right now that bookers are not, in all probability, human. Any human traits have likely disappeared through the process of natural selection.

Being non-, sub- or unhuman, they have no knowledge or understanding of your act, or even a point of view. Thus, an urban Jewish comic may get booked at a KKK cross burning for twenty-five dollars, bus fare and all the pork you can eat. Don't be surprised if it happens to you.

But let's take comedian X and follow him through a typical, generic road engagement.

The Booking Agent's Call

"I got you three weeks at Spleen-Bursts in Nowheresville, Idabama, and then a month and a half at Gurgles in Pre-Evolution, East Dakota."

A good manager must understand comedy, not just how to make travel arrangements. When you pick a manager, be sure he or she thinks in terms of your total career, not just a quick buck. A comedy career builds from point to point, from your first booking step-by-step to your own HBO special.

A good manager should:

1. Be able to discuss new material with you.
2. Be decisive.
3. Know when to take a job and when *not* to take a job.
4. Make sure that everything runs smoothly: from your life on the road to your bookings to your press and media coverage.

The road: In the early stages of your career you should play *anywhere.* It's a good way to build a following. If you play twenty times in Cleveland (and you're funny), soon you'll have people who want to see you again—and who'll bring their friends.

Travel Arrangements

"You'll be flying Uniwing Airlines, the company that says, 'One wing is more than enough.' Their motto is 'We land in parking lots.'"

Accommodations

"You'll be staying at the club owner's luxurious condo, which he or she has graciously provided at a cost of only twice what they're paying you."

The Club

The architectural environment is often designed to enhance the self-esteem and the performance level of the artist.

After the Show

You are formally introduced to an attractive doyenne of local society, who exposes you to the rich cultural heritage of her particular region (e.g., Idaho Potato Gonorrhea).

Trying to Get Paid

The owner of the club is often involved
in other businesses or charitable
enterprises that may divert him from his
duties as a comedy entrepreneur.

The End of the Engagement

Bid a fond farewell to this quaint little
burg, and count the days until you
return in triumph.

chapter

11

KNOW YOUR AUDIENCE

Sizing up an audience is one of the comic's most important critical faculties. Here's a test: We're going to put you onstage in front of various types of audiences with three jokes. See if you choose the one that's right for each audience.

1. "I just flew in from Miami and, boy, are my arms tired."
2. "A bum walks up to me in the street, says, 'I haven't had a bite in a week.' So I bit him."
3. "I really relate to some of your progressive ideas. I like to let my buddies gang-bang my girlfriend and then urinate on her. That's real cool, ya grease monkeys."

1. "I just flew in from Miami and, boy, are my arms tired."
2. "A bum walks up to me in the street, says, 'I haven't had a bite in a week.' So I bit him."
3. "I'm sure you do a lot of things here that you'd be proud to tell your children—like balling hookers and throwing water bags out the hotel window."

1. "I just flew in from Miami and, boy, are my arms tired."
2. "A bum walks up to me in the street, says, 'I haven't had a bite in a week.' So I bit him."
3. "Spend twelve grand a year for tuition so you can drink yourselves into a coma and forget everything you've learned. Real smart. Why don't you have, like, thirty more beers and then drive on the wrong side of the road. Make your parents proud."

1. "I just flew in from Miami and boy, are my arms tired."
2. "A bum walks up to me in the street, says, 'I haven't had a bite in a week.' So I bit him."
3. "Do you guys want me to take a couple of minutes' break so you can go to the phone and squeal on each other? Or put bombs under each other's car? It's all right with me. I could use a drink, anyway."

chapter 12

NEWMAN'S NOTE

Try not to open for a heavy-metal act!

HOW TO BE
AN OPENING ACT

Before you reach the pinnacle of success—star billing—you may have to endure the humiliation and degradation of being an opening act. There are four basic acts that you might have to open for. Let's examine and analyze them so you'll be assured of success within your demeaning little slot.

TYPE OF ACT	WHAT THE STAR PERFORMER WANTS	WHAT THE AUDIENCE WANTS
1. Singer	Don't upstage me	Get off the stage
2. Specialty act	Don't upstage me	Get off the stage
3. A more famous comedian	Don't upstage me	Get off the stage
4. Rock group	Kill time	Get off the stage or die

In order to be successful, you will be forced to adapt your act, not just for the audiences, but for the different environments in which you'll be performing. Here are some good tips for these different venues:

Intimacy Doesn't Work in a Stadium.

© 1983, MELISSA HAYES ENGLISH/PHOTO RESEARCHERS

"And now I'd like to do my pinky mime routine."

Don't Criticize Alcohol or Organized Crime in a Nightclub.

"You know what's really ruining this country? Drunks . . . and the Mafia!"

In a TV Studio,
Don't Play to the Technicians.

"Excuse me, sir. You with the camera.
What do you do for a living? Sir? Sir!"

chapter

You know, writing a book is hard work. Not like being a comedian. If you think this book stuff is so easy, *you* write a chapter. *Really. Go ahead.* Here, for your comedic enlightenment, are several useful experiments, personally prepared by your Belzerness, to enhance your capacity for this awesome chore. We've even provided a few blank pages. Knock yourself out. I'm taking a break this chapter. Call me when it's over. And, please, no cheating.

1. Write three one-liners about your wife, girl-friend, husband or boyfriend.
2. Write a short, one-minute monologue about your childhood.
3. Work on an impression of a celebrity, not including James Cagney, Edward G. Robinson or Humphrey Bogart.
4. If you are so inclined, find a prop that will inspire you to great heights.

chapter

15

The classic setting for a comedian's performance remains the nightclub. Let me take you on a guided tour of one nightclub so that when you play one someday (yeah, *right*) you'll know what to expect. Come on . . . stay with me, because I'm a big celebrity.

First we encounter the doorman. His job is to guide patrons in and keep the riff-raff out . . .

BELZER: "Hi, Tony."

DOORMAN: "My name is Steve. And where do you think you're going?"

BELZER: "Hey, don't you recognize me?"

DOORMAN: "No, I never go to the circus."

BELZER: "Well, do you recognize *this?*"

DOORMAN: "Have a nice evening, sir."

Next we encounter the maître d'. He
    orchestrates the seating
    arrangements for the nightclub.
    BELZER: "Table for two, please."
    MAÎTRE D': "Where's the other member
    of your party?"
    BELZER: "Out there. The other member
    of my party is the reader."
    MAÎTRE D': "The reader?"
    BELZER: "Yeah, you see, we're in a
    book and . . . oh, forget it."

Perhaps this is a good time to examine
seating patterns in a nightclub:

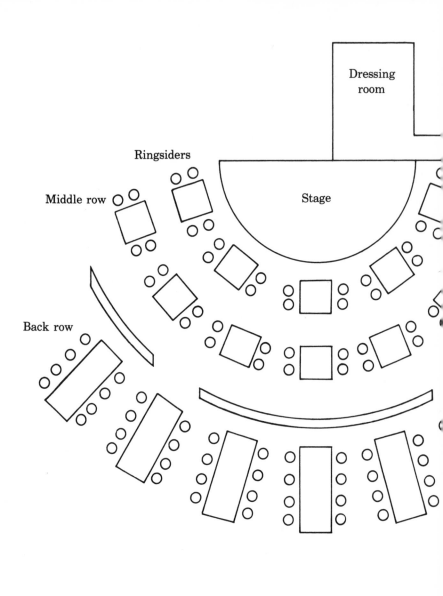

Kitchen

Ringsiders: Loud; love to be part of the show, like to be abused; masochists—you can steal their drinks and cigarettes. They drink beer by the pitcher.

Middle row: Middle-of-the-roaders: conventioneers, large groups, first-dates; the section most likely to heckle; generally a group you wouldn't want to hang out with. The drunkest; they drink hard liquor.

Back row: They think they're better and smarter than you—and funnier; to prove it, they sit in darkness and don't laugh; usually unattractive and bitter; won't take a chance at heckling for fear they'll be topped and humiliated. Too sober—Perrier and soft drinks.

There's only *one* sacred cow in the
comedy business: FRANCIS ALBERT SINATRA

*Rule number one of the
comedy business:* Never, never,
ever make fun of Frank.

Dead comics tell no jokes, if you get my drift. But occasionally you'll find yourself on a roll, and out pops a great line about the Chairman of the Board. There is one and *only* one course of action and it must be taken immediately. Utter the phrase that has kept Don Rickles from doing his act with a respirator instead of a microphone. This is your only chance of avoiding a painful and slow death. Say it now to yourself and memorize it: "Just kidding, Frank."

Say it again: "Just kidding, Frank."

Now that wasn't too bad, was it? Other than this, I'm happy to report there are no sacred cows in comedy.

JIM McHUGH/SYGMA

Just to prove there are no other sacred cows, let's make
fun of God . . .

"Nice robe, God, whaddya just wake up?
They've invented a new thing since the
dawn of time, God babe, they call it a
razor. What are you, God, like five
thousand years old now? Don't get much
'cosmic nookie' anymore, huh? Blows
that 'eternal orgasm' theory out
of the water, huh, God?"

NEWMAN'S NOTE

If you're a funny performer you should try to create your own material. But you are allowed to buy material from comedy writers. (At the very least, take the writer out to dinner.) In fact, writing comedy routines is a good way to start in this business.

DIFFERENT TYPES OF COMEDIANS

There are as many different types of comedians as there are, well, different types of comedians.

So, with that in mind, we thought it would be useful to give you a brief overview of the various categories so that you might find your niche with greater ease.

Remember: If you don't fit into any of these categories, don't worry, just get out of the business, okay, babe?

The Woman Comedian

"All the men I date have one thing in common, they have no dicks . . ."

The Black Comedian

"My dick is so big . . ."

The Jewish Comic

"Even my dick is in therapy . . ."

The Ventriloquist

"What's it like having a wooden dick?"

The Southern Comedian

"And my pa says, 'Son, that's not the pig's tail, it's his dick!'"

The Singing Comedian

" 'Ode to My Dick.' "

The Impressionist

"If Jack Nicholson were a dick, ladies and gentlemen . . ."

The "Prop" Comedian

"King Kong's dick."

The Foreign Comedian

"In my country, the word for *dick* is . . ."

The "Observation" Comic

"Have you ever noticed your dick . . . ?"

The Comedy Team

"Who's dick's on first . . ."

The Belz, babe . . .

NEWMAN'S NOTE

Make sure you develop *one absolutely funny minute* as part of your routine. That way, when you audition, you'll be sure to be remembered. Even if the rest of your material isn't up to that standard, whoever you're auditioning for will still remember that you were funny.

THE TRAPPINGS
OF SUCCESS

Being a comedian is more than being funny. In some cases it's being a completely insufferable egomaniac. And that means, yes . . . an entourage.

Now granted, the young comic, doing freebies at the campus pub, might look a tad foolish with an entourage, but for the successful phenom it's *de rigueur*.

How does one acquire an entourage? Well, the sweet smell of moolah attracts an entourage like manure attracts flies.

What does today's entourage consist of? Let's see, shall we?

THE BODYGUARD

THE GROUPIES

THE YESMAN

THE MANAGER

144 ∎

The Bodyguard: He's mean, he's bad, and *if* he's willing to take a bullet in the head for three hundred bucks a week, he's dumb.

The Yes Man: The Yes Man makes the comic look brilliant by doubling over in convulsive laughter every time the comic emits even the most inane utterance.

The Manager: He doesn't even find the comic amusing, but he enjoys wearing out calculator batteries figuring out how much money the comic makes.

The Groupies: These are the babes, the bimbos, the comedy groupies. Let's face facts: Eddie Murphy attracts one kind of woman and Louie Anderson another, so think about that when you're deciding on an image.

If you should become highly successful in the world of comedy, you'll be forced to indulge in the trappings of success. Your choices, quite apart from your material or delivery, may decide the course of your career.

So, here are a couple of hints from your old pal, the Belz.

The Proper Home

The pattern has always been that a comedian would become a star in New York, then buy a house in Hollywood or Beverly Hills. Lenny Bruce lived in the Hollywood Hills; Jay Leno bought Charlie Chaplin's house. The trend is to buy a dead comedian's house; that way you have the aura of the dead comedian's material—*and* you have a house. Success is not just getting your own house, but getting a house that was owned by someone funnier than you. And more famous. And richer. I recently purchased Moms Mabley's palatial estate.

Sometimes comedians fall into the trap of sharing a home with another comedian. This is taboo if you really want to appear successful. Because even if it's a nice house, people will say, "Oh, he has to share the rent." Never have a roommate. Live alone. Even if you're lonely. You're better off having the whole *Citizen Kane/Xanadu* scene than living with another comic. *Never* have a roommate.

The Proper Automobile

The key decision in choosing a car is something low to the ground. Cars that are high off the ground are for clerks, not comics. Now, sure, in your salad days, when you had no money, you would've driven anything, even a Yugo. But as a successful comedian you must own or lease a fine, low-slung automobile. Some stars like tinted windows, but not comics—they like being recognized.

The Proper Spouse
You want a woman who, essentially, is too good for you. You want a woman who thinks you're funny but doesn't laugh at *everything* you say, like, "Honey, I'm having chest pains . . ."

She doesn't have to think you're the funniest man on the face of the earth, but she shouldn't think somebody else is either. She should also trust you when you go out on the road, even though she shouldn't.

Comics should never date other comics. When you split up, it's very messy. Who gets custody of the material? She gets the material during the week and you get to use it on weekends and holidays? It just doesn't work.

The Proper Career Direction
A successful comedian usually becomes more megalomaniacal as the success barometer rises. Initial success might be achieved from stand-up but then the comedian envisions a sitcom, then a two-picture deal, and then Broadway, albums, extended tours, Europe, and then his or her own production company. These things are all fine. Don't do dinner theater. Don't open stuff, like shopping centers or bowling alleys. Don't do fairs, especially if you follow the pig contest.

chapter

20

COMEDY AROUND THE WORLD

Comedy is universal. Just ask Rich Little; *no one* thinks he's funny. But although there are basic commonalities that we all share, it's the specific differences of each culture that, when exploited for comedy purposes, often yield the best results.

So come on, let's take "The Belz Tour of Comedy Around the World" and watch carefully as I suddenly gear my material to my audience.

"And the other guy says, I'll show ya
how to sharpen your spear . . ."

"And the Jew says: 'Medium rare . . .' "

"So the Eskimo says: 'You club the baby seal and I'll get the whale fat . . .' "

© BETTYE LANE/PHOTO RESEARCHERS

". . . and the Reform Jew chokes to death on a tefillin . . ."

"And Allah says: 'You drove the truck into the wrong embassy.'"

"And the dissident says: 'Chernobyl is bad, but Vegas is worse.'"

"And he says: 'I miss Custer, let's get drunk.'"

"And the Earthling says: 'I thought *we* were the smartest species.'"

You may have read the first twenty
chapters of this book and said, "Sure, it's
a classic, Belz, and I understand where
you're coming from, bro, but I just
don't know if I have what it takes
to be a professional comedian."
Let me say, first of all, don't *ever*
talk to me in that tone of voice.
Secondly, keep your day job, babe.
Thirdly, you *have* come a long way, you

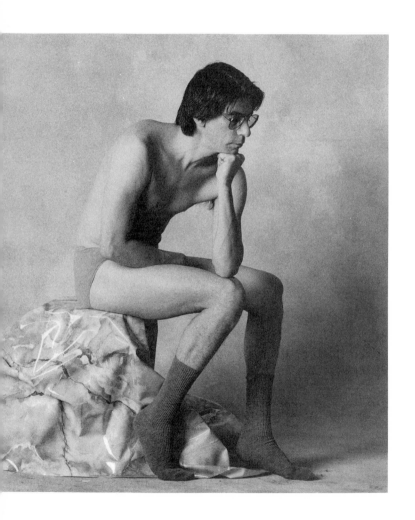

little grasshopper you. You've absorbed the lessons we have taught you. You have learned about the material world of stand-up comedy. But now, it is time for your initiation; now it's time to learn the spiritual side of stand-up—the fire that must burn within you. This is a rite of passage. These are the comedian's five stages of death:

Getting Heckled: You never see it coming. You're onstage, trying desperately to remember what you're going to say next, when you are interrupted. Stopped dead. Train of thought derailed. Someone has broken your rhythm. The rhythm of your act. The rhythm of your heart. You've been heckled . . .

Getting Topped: Sweat glistens on your forehead and upper lip. Your blood pressure rises. Your shoes and crotch get moist. You swiftly and appropriately respond to the heckler's unwarranted intrusion. Your comeback is quick, clever, to the point. For a brief moment, you regain your composure. You're cocky, self-assured. But you failed to win the audience. You lost their sympathy. Amazingly, they cheer and applaud when the heckler answers your comeback. It is anarchy. A revolution.

A coup d'état. And you are the leader of the old regime.

Getting Booed: Desperately you utter something that one person, or an entire group, takes issue with. Perhaps it is only their drunken muddled interpretation of what you've said, but that doesn't matter now. They have emitted that noise—that resonant, guttural utterance. You feel like the little pig whose home gets blown down by the big, bad wolf: chilled . . . naked. The boo—that burst of frigid air—envelops you. For a moment, a brief moment, you die. You freeze to death . . .

Bombing: Your balls (or ovaries) retreat into your stomach, where your heart also is currently residing. You hear your voice, but it doesn't seem to be coming from your mouth. You are buried deep within your own body, which is nothing more than a corporeal shell. The audience stares at you, awkwardly, uncomfortably—like you're a car crash; like you're the Elephant Man. Suddenly, religion seems like a good idea. "Oh, please, Lord, help me through this horror. This veritable hell on earth. Please, Lord, I'll never   [fill in the blank]   again . . ."

Recovery: You say something. Then,

something else. You don't know what.
You don't know where it comes from.
You're possessed by comic demons.
You're channeling for ancient comedians.
But, it causes titters, which move rapidly
through the audience like a glorious
virus that grows progressively worse
until it develops into a laugh, a guffaw,
rolling in the aisles, choking gagging
laughter and applause and, oh, glory be!
you've won them back! "Oh, thank you,
Lord, even though I'm still an atheist!
Love is everywhere! You've been a great
audience. Good night."

Anytime during your performance, during the course
of your entire career, you may experience any or all of
these stages.

Know them well—they *are* comedy.

NEWMAN'S NOTE

You never want to die, you always want to kill.

NEWMAN'S NOTE

IMPORTANT DEFINITIONS

Killing: When your material was so good, you blew the roof off the ceiling and maybe even got a standing ovation.
Dying: When your material goes into the toilet.
Toilet: Someplace you don't want your material to go in.

NEWMAN'S NOTE

Everyone blanks out, forgets the joke in the middle of telling it. Don't try to stumble around and complete your thought. Go immediately to something else—even if your transition makes no sense.

chapter

22

YOUR COMIC PERSONA

Congratulations! You're ready to leap across the void from your humdrum, mundane, everyday existence to being a stand-up comic. (Yeah, sure, like this book really *helped* you.) Anyway, welcome to the wish-book chapter, where you get to choose the elements that make up your comic persona.

The Look

Before an audience hears you, they *see* you. With that in mind, please be careful as you choose one:

1. T-shirt and jeans
2. A suit
3. A bad suit
4. A bad haircut
5. Mismatched pants and shirt
6. Pants too short
7. Hat or cap
8. Brightly colored shoes or sneakers
9. T-shirt with funny saying
10. A goofy costume:
    a. Adult diaper
    b. Surgical gown
    c. Prop clothes
11. Distracting jewelry

The Hook (aka the Gimmick)

After they see you, they're going to hear you. So now it's time to choose a "hook" that will be easily recognized and a catchphrase that will be often repeated.

1. Work with food
2. Bad language
3. Work with guitar (or other instrument)

4. Misogynist
   5. Man-hater
   6. Fat
   7. Bald
   8. Annoying laugh
   9. Steal everybody else's act
  10. Screams
  11. Funny name

The Catchphrase

   1. "Don't point that thing at me."
   2. "I just got here myself."
   3. "Oh no, not me again."
   4. "It's not my occupation."
   5. "Ni-tro-*glycerin!!*"
   6. "I'm treated with utter disrespect."
   7. "Don't call me Pinky."
   8. "Whoops!"
   9. "Are we able to converse?"
  10. "Good night, and may (deity of your choice) bless."

chapter

23

LIST OF FUNNY WORDS, PHRASES, ETC.

Five Funny Words: dreidel, diaphanous, phlegm, stevedore, spatula

Five Funny States: Wyoming, South Dakota, Kentucky, New Jersey, Arkansas

Five Funny Body Parts: pancreas, spleen, liver, rectum, earlobe

Five Funny Numbers: 12; 806; 94,312; 6,000,011; and, of course, 22

Five Funny Countries: Cameroon, Lichtenstein, Canada, Lapland, and, of course, Sri Lanka

chapter 24

Well, congratulations. You've made it through what may very well be the most important book you'll ever skim, if I may, in all modesty, say so myself or speaking for Rick and Larry, if we may say so ourselves. You're probably drained right now. Your mind is spinning, you're trying to digest the overwhelming amount of wisdom, information, insight, and, yes, comfort that only a book like this—hey, only *this* book could provide.

. . . Yeah, right, right, sure, sure, uh huh, *right*. . . Like, they're taking all the Bibles out of the motels and replacing them with this book. Okay, so it's not the Bible. But, does the Bible have pictures? No! More important, does the Bible have the Belz, your spirit guide to the netherworld of humor? No! It is an indisputable fact that nowhere in the Bible, or the Koran for that matter, am I mentioned even *once!* An oversight? Perhaps. Regardless, I'm all over *this* book, and that's what counts.

If you're standing in a bookstore right now, debating with yourself whether to be a big spender and shell out a measly $13.95 for this endless wealth of literary brilliance or to be a cheap son of a bitch, remember three things:

1. This is the funniest book ever written.
2. It makes a great gift.
3. I have a very materialist, consumerist family to support. They like new, shiny expensive things—things that only a best-selling author can afford.

Now, let's say you've decided to buy the book, or you've already made the purchase (snicker, snicker). Let me strongly advise buying a second or even a third copy. Why? Well, put your ear up against the page, and I'll explain. If you were to lose your *only* copy of this book, you would be so distraught, so inconsolable, that you would plunge into a deep black depression from which you would never emerge, and frankly, I don't need that kind of pressure.

Well, I—we—hope you've enjoyed this book. I hope it's been useful and provided a few chuckles. Why don't more authors do this? Can you imagine Norman Mailer thanking you for reading his fat fucking book? Or, Stephen King saying, "Hey, I hope I scared the shit out of you."

Anyway, I hope the next time we meet, it'll be on stage at one of the myriad comedy clubs spread out across this great land of ours. And if you see me at one of these clubs, come on up to me and say, "Belz, thanks, thanks a million." And, I'll probably say, "Thank *this,* babe!" Then, I'll brush past you, climb into my limo, go back to my luxurious hotel suite, humiliate a whore, and cry myself to sleep.

Thank you, good night, and drive safely . . .

CAMEOS, GUEST-STARS AND CREDITS

Photos by Anthony Loew
Makeup by Laura Geller
Stylist: Elizabeth Minetree
Extras: Richard Aquan, Tracy Dene, Jeffrey Dene, Robert
    Dene, Michael Di Paolo
The Belz's wardrobe by Howard Behar
Special thanks to Howard and Terrance
Also, thanks to Gene Roseman, president of Flaunt Models
Clothes from the Antique Boutique, 714 Broadway New York
    City
Special thanks to Lara and Albert
And special acknowledgments to:
    Sophie Wengrod
    Barbara DeSantis
    Adam Leslie
    Wendy Bass
    Harlee McBride
    Bree Benton
    Jessica Benton
    Kitten and Smokey

BEAT: A rest space, between setup and punch line, between lines of a routine or between various routines, taken purely for comic effect.

BOMB (BOMBING; DYING; INTO THE TOILET): When a comedian's presentation receives a complete and utter lack of response from the audience.

COMEBACK: A response to a heckler.

DELIVERY: The style or manner with which you perform your material.

HUNK (ROUTINE, BIT): A series of jokes on a single theme.

KILL (KNOCK 'EM DEAD; KICK ASS): The antithesis of bombing, the audience finds your every remark and gesture hysterically, unbelievably, uncontrollably funny.

MONOLOGUE: Can be the same as *hunk* or can encompass the sum total of your various routines. Your act.

APPENDIX I.
GLOSSARY

ONE-LINER: A short joke containing setup and punch line in the same sentence or paragraph.

PROP: The enemy of wit; an apparatus or object used for the specific purpose of engendering laughter; can be handled or worn, or simply pointed out; can be a natural part of the environment or a contrivance.

PUNCH LINE (PAYOFF; BLOW; CAPPER; SNAPPER; BUTTON): The humorous portion, usually found at the end of a joke.

SETUP (STRAIGHT LINE): The body of the joke; the information necessary to understand the punch line.

TAKE: A sudden look in one direction or another, using the head, or the entire body, either in response to something you've said or to an offstage remark or sound. Often, immediately repeated.

TIMING: . . . is everything; the secret of comedy.

Many of these clubs have amateur or showcase nights.

Alabama

The Comedy Club
430 Green Springs Hwy.,
Suite 28, Homewood
(205) 942-0008

Alaska

P.J.'s Comedy Alley
3606 Spenard Rd., Anchorage
(907) 561-9017

Arizona

Finney Bones
4821 N. Scottsdale Rd., Scottsdale

The Comedy Zone at Cafe Napoli
1060 N. Craycroft, Tucson
(602) 74-JOKES

Arkansas

The Comedy House
Breckenrodge Village, Little Rock
(501) 221-2004

Zanies Comedy Showcase
110500 W. Markham, Little Rock
(501) 376-1853

California

Nantucket Fish Co.
123 First St., Bernicia
(707) 745-2233

Remingtons
1730 West Campbell, Campbell
(408) 370-3280

The Top Flight
303 Main St., Chico

Laughs Unlimited
Birdcage Walk, 5957 Sunrise
 Blvd., Citrus Heights
(916) 962-1559

Laff Stop
415 Foothill Blvd., Claremont
(714) 621-6808

Tommy T's
1655 Willow Pass Rd., Concord
(415) 686-LAFF

Tres Hombres
1400 Willow Pass Rd., Concord
(415) 825-2626

APPENDIX II.
COMEDY CLUBS
AROUND THE COUNTRY

Fat Fanny's
103A Town and Country Dr.,
  Danville
(415) 838-0606

L.A. Cabaret
17271 Ventura Blvd., Encino
(818) 501-3737

Hot Rod Cafe
39148 State St., Fremont
(415) 793-5491

Bogie's
764 "P" Street, Fresno

Comedy and Magic Store
1018 Hermosa Ave., Hermosa
  Beach
(213) 372-1193

Niles Station
37501 Niles Blvd., Fremont
(415) 794-7977

Miramar Beach Inn
Miramar, Half Moon Bay
(415) 726-4143

Casa Carlitas
24041 Southland Dr., Hayward

Tommy T's Comedy and Sports
  Bar
24744 Mission Blvd., Hayward
(415) 881-4789

The Comedy Store
9433 Sunset Blvd., Hollywood
(213) 656-6225

The Improv
8162 Melrose Ave., Hollywood
(213) 651-2583

The Comedy Store
916 Pearl, La Jolla
(619) 454-9176

Cobbs Pub at The Cannery
2801 Leavenworth St., San
  Francisco
(415) 928-4320

The Comedy Club
111 W. Pine, Long Beach
(213) 437-5326

Igby's
11637 Tennessee Place, Los
  Angeles
(213) 477-3553

No One Broadway
102 S. Santa Cruz Ave., Los Gatos

Hop Singh's
4110 Lincoln Blvd., Marina Del
  Ray

Sweetriver Saloon
510 Merced Mall, Merced
(209) 383-5542

The Club
321 D. Alvarado, Paso de
  Alvarado Bldg., Monterey
(408) 646-9244

Sports Page
1431 Stierlin Rd., N., Mountain
  View
(415) 961-1992

Napa Valley Comedy Cafe
1040 Clinton St., Napa
(707) 252-4952

Brookside Cafe
5989 Mowry Ave., Newark
(415) 796-5700

The Laff Stop
2122 SE Bristol, Newport Beach
(714) 852-8762

Bay Area Laugh Factory
1736 Franklin St., Oakland
(415) 334-3894

Club International
1229 23rd Avenue, Oakland

Hyatt International Hotel
455 Hegenberger, Oakland

Laughs Unlimited
1124 Firehouse Alley, Old
  Sacramento
(916) 446-5905

The Improv
832 Garnet Ave., Pacific Beach
(619) 483-4520

The Ice House
24 N. Mentor, Pasadena
(818) 577-1894

Sunshine Saloon
1807 Santa Rita Rd., Pleasanton
(415) 846-6108

Tampico Kitchen
822 Pacific Ave., Santa Cruz
(408) 423-2240

Cobb's Comedy Club
The Cannery, San Francisco
(415) 928-4320

Holy City Zoo
408 Clement St., San Francisco
(415) 641-4242

Lipps
201 9th St. (at Howard), San
  Francisco
(415) 552-3466

Other Cafe
100 Carl St., San Francisco
(415) 681-0748

Punch Line
444 A Battery St., San Francisco
(415) 474-3801

Tommy T's
150 W. Juana, San Leandro
(415) 351-LAFF

Center Stage Comedy Club
23 N. Market, San Jose
(408) 298-2266

94th Aero Squadron
1160 Coleman Avenue, San Jose
(408) 287-6150

The Last Laugh
29 N. Pedro St., San Jose

Toppers
4400 Stevens Creek Blvd., San Jose
(408) 247-7795

Bob Zany's Comedy Outlet at Wm. Randolph's
1850 Monterey St., San Luis Obispo
(805) 543-3333

Bob Zany's Comedy Outlet at Bombay's
4223 State St., Santa Barbara
(805) 682-8689

Bob Zany's Comedy Outlet at Silver Dollar Saloon
213 E. Main St., Santa Maria
(805) 925-1193

New George's
342 4th St., San Rafael
(415) 457-1515

Daily Planet
120 5th St., Santa Rosa
(707) 578-1205

Studio Kafé
418 Mendocino Ave., Santa Rosa
(707) 523-1971

Sweetriver Saloon
248 Coddington Center, Santa Rosa
(707) 526-0400

Victorian Oak House
230 Mt. Hermon Rd., Scotts Valley
(408) 438-5903

Rooster T. Feathers
157 W. El Camino Real, Sunnyvale
(408) 736-0921

Laughs Unlimited
4555 N. Pershine, Stockton
(209) 951-LAFF

The Comedy Store
333 Universal Terrace Parkway, Universal City
(818) 980-1212, ext. 6112

Bob Zany's Comedy Outlet at Reuben's
299 S. Moorpark Rd., Thousand Oaks
(805) 495-0431

Harris House
350 Butcher Road, Vacaville

Bob Zany's Comedy Outlet at Club Soda
317 E. Main St., Ventura
(805) 652-1164

Punch Line
1220 Petticoat Lane, Walnut Creek
(415) 935-2002

Bob Zany's Comedy Outlet at
Lampost Pizza
2431 Azusa Ave., West Covina
(818) 964-4341

The Laff Factory
8001 Sunset Blvd., West
Hollywood
(213) 656-8960
(Note: Monday is Ladies' Comedy
Night

Colorado
Jeff Valdez Comedy Corner
204 N. Union, Colorado Springs
(303) 578-0496

Comedy Works
1226 15th St., Denver
(303) 595-3637

George McKelvey's Comedy Club
7225 East Hampden, Denver
(303) 758-5275

Comedy Works
7 Olde Town Square, Suite 144,
Fort Collins
(303) 221-5481

Connecticut
Billy Jack Café of Comedy
53 Wells St., Glastonbury

The Treehouse Café and Comedy
Club
1575 Post Rd., Westport

Delaware
The Comedy Cabaret
410 Market St., Wilmington
(302) 652-6873

Florida
Ron Bennington's Comedy Line
2560 U.S. 19 N., Clearwater
(813) 785-8412 (bookings)

Mac's Famous Bar
2000 S. Atlantic, Daytona Beach
(904) 252-9239

The Funny Bone Comedy Club
401 2nd St. E., Indian Rocks
Beach
(813) 596-4666

The Comic Strip
1432 N. Federal Hwy., Fort
Lauderdale
(305) 565-8867

Bijou Comedy Club
1994 San Carlos Blvd., Fort
Meyers Beach

TZ's on the Narrows
401 Second Street E., Indian Rocks
Beach
(813) 593-0716

Bonkers Comedy Club
4315 N. Orange Blossom Tr.,
Orlando
(305) 948-NUTS

The Comedy Corner
2000 S. Dixie, W. Palm Beach

The Comedy Corner
3447 W. Kennedy, Tampa

The Comedy Spot
Sheraton Miracle Mile Inn,
Panama City Beach

The Comedy Club (located in the
Ramada Inn Airport)
6545 N. Tamiami Trail, (U.S. 41),
Sarasota

Mainstreet Comedy Club
4800 S. Cleveland Ave., Fort
Myers
(813) 936-FUNY

Coconuts Comedy Club
16601 NW 2nd Ave., N. Miami
(305) 948-NUTS

Coconuts Comedy Club
6110 Gulf Blvd., St. Petersburg
Beach
(813) 360-7935

Coconuts Comedy Club
2 Minute Man Cosway, Cocoa
Beach
(305) 783-0955

Georgia
Punch Line
280 Hilldebrand Dr., Atlanta
(404) 252-LAFF

Slapstix
1325 Virginia, Atlanta

Idaho
Peabody's
300 S. 24th St., Coeur d'Alene
(208) 667-9057

The University Inn
1516 Pullman Rd., Moscow
(208) 882-0550

Illinois
Comedy On Tap at Jay Wendell's
Saloon and Eatery
24 East Miner St., Arlington
Heights

The Wacko's Comedy Club
312 W. Roosevelt, Berwyn

Zanies
1538 North Wells St., Chicago

Roar's West at Firgates
25250 W. Lakeshore Dr., Ingleside

Comedy Womb
8030 W. Ogden Ave. (above Pines
Rest.), Lyons
(312) 442-5755

Zanies Comedy Nite Club
2200 S. Elmhurst Rd., Mt.
Prospect
(312) 228-6166

Bill Brady's Comedy Capers at
Barrel of Laughs
10345 So. Central Ave., Oak Lawn
(312) 499-2969

The Funnybone Comedy Club
1725 Algonquin Rd., Schaumburg
(312) 303-5700

Comedy Cottage at the Hilton
Speakeasy
700 East Adams, Springfield
(217) 789-1530

Comedy Cottage
9751 W. Higgins Rd., Rosemont
(312) 696-4077

Comedy Cottage West
1100 W. Lake St. Roselle
(312) 696-4077

Roars North at The Grand Slam
1340 Grand Ave., Waukegan

Indiana
Snickerz
5629 St. Joe Rd., Fort Wayne
(219) 486-0216

Crackers
8702 Keystone Crossing,
 Indianapolis
(317) 846-2500

Indianapolis Comedy Connection
247 South Meridan St.,
 Indianapolis
(317) 631-3536

Holiday Star Comedy Club
U.S. 30 & I 65, Merriville

Bros Comedy Company at Center
 St. Blues Cafe
229 S. Michigan St., South Bend
(219) 237-5007 or 288-0245

Iowa
Hollywood's Comedy Club
209 1st Ave. SE, Cedar Rapids
(319) 362-8133

The Redwood Restaurant Ltd.
3809 109th St., Urbandale
(515) 276-1721/1712; 276-3035
 (bookings)

Kansas
Bushwackers Comedy Invasion
531 North Manhattan, Manhattan
(913) 539-4321

Kentucky
The Funny Bone Comedy Club
600 W. 3rd St., Covington

Comedy on Broadway
146 N. Broadway, Lexington
(606) 259-0013

The Funny Farm at the Mid-City
 Mall
1250 Bardstown Rd., Louisville
(317) 846-2500

Louisiana
The Funny Bone Comedy Club
4715 Bennington, Baton Rouge
(504) 928-9996

Jodie's Comedy Shop
4000 Industrial Dr., Bossier City

The Punch Line
4704 Veterans Blvd., New Orleans
(504) 454-7973

Maryland
Charm City Comedy Club
102 Water St., Baltimore
(301) 576-8558

Comedy Factory Outlet
Lombard and Light St., Baltimore
(301) LAF-FTER

Massachusetts
Comedy Connection
76 Warrenton St., Boston
(617) 426-6339

Dick Doherty's Comedy Vault at
  Remington's of Boston
124 Boylston St., Boston
(617) 267-6626

Nick's Comedy Shop
100 Warrenton St., Boston
(617) 482-0930

Play It Again, Sam
1314 Commonwealth Ave., Boston
(617) 232-4242

Stitches
969 Commonwealth Ave., Boston
(617) 972-6000 ext. 5233

Catch a Rising Star
30 JFK St., Harvard Sq.,
  Cambridge
(617) 661-9887

Stevie D's Comedy Tonight
261 N. Main St., Rt. 114,
  Middleton
(508) 777-1778

The Upstairs Club
256 Elm St., Westfield
(413) 527-2529

Michigan
Heidelberg's Comedy on Main St.
215 N. Main, Ann Arbor
(313) 995-8888

Main Street Comedy Showcase
314 East Liberty St., Ann Arbor
(313) 996-9080

Comedy Castle
2593 Woodward Ave., Berkeley
(313) 542-9900

Bea's Comedy Kitchen
541 E. Larned, Detroit
(313) 961-2581

Groucho's Comedy
1318 Ledington, Escanaba
(906) 786-2531

Chaplin's
34244 Groesback Hwy., Fraser
(313) 739-6628

Comedy Den
2845 Thornhills SE, Grand Rapids
(616) 949-9322

The 1891 Room Comedy Club
110 Battle Alley, Holly
(313) 634-1891

The Hilton Comedy Club
Kalamazoo Center
100 W. Michigan Ave.,
  Kalamazoo

Zanies Comedy Nite Club
404 S. Burdick, Kalamazoo
(616) 344-5400

Connxtions Comedy Club
2900 N.E. Street, Lansing
(517) 482-1468

The Comedy Crossing
23055 Telegraph Rd., Southfield
(313) 353-3798

Traverse City Comedy Club
738 S. Garfield, Traverse City
(616) 941-0988

Minnesota
Belly Laffs at the Mandarin Yen
  Restaurant
494 and Penn, Bloomington
(612) 888-8900

Comedy Gallery
1028 LaSalle Ave., Minneapolis
(612) 339-9031

David Wood's Rib Tickler
716 North 1st St., Minneapolis
(612) 339-9031

Missouri
Deja Vu's Comedy Night Live
701 Cherry St., Columbia
(314) 443-3216

The Funny Bone Comedy Club
1148 W. 103rd, Kansas City
(816) 941-YUKS

Stanford and Sons Comedy House
543 Westport Rd., Kansas City
(816) 753-JOKE

Off the Wall Comedy Club
3303 S. Campbell, Springfield
(417) 882-4424

The Funny Bone Comedy Club
940 Westport Plaza, St. Louis
(314) 469-6692

The Funny Bone Comedy Club
19 Ronnie's Plaza, St. Louis
(314) 469-6692

Montana
Park Place
2621 Brooks, Missoula
(406) 721-9359

Nebraska
The Riverside Ballroom
Johnny Carson Blvd., Norfolk
(402) 371-9961; (702) 276-3035
  (bookings)

Nevada
Dunes Hotel & Country Club
3650 Las Vegas Blvd. S., Las
  Vegas
(702) 737-4110

Caesar's Tahoe
Crystal Cabaret, Stateline
(702) 588-3515

New Jersey
Cherry Hill Comedy Cabaret
Hyatt Cherry Hill, Rt. 70 &
  Cuthbert Blvd., Cherry Hill
(609) 665-6581

Wall Street Comedy Stop
1050 Wall St. West, Lyndhurst

Mitchell's Comedy Cafe
5 W. Broad St., Palmyra
(609) 829-3161

Rascals
425 Pleasant Valley Way, W.
  Orange
(201) 736-2726

New Mexico
Duke City Comedy Speakeasy at
  Carrdio's Pizza
108 Vassar SE
(505) 255-7831

Laffs
3100 Juan Tohe, NE Albuquerque
(505) 296-5653

New York
Governors Comedy Shop
Division Ave., Levittown
(516) 731-3358

Chuckle's Comedy Club
139 Jericho Turnpike, Mineola
(718) 934-0596

Caroline's
332 Eighth Ave., New York
(212) 924-3499

Catch a Rising Star
1487 First Ave., New York
(212) 794-1906

The Comedy House
48 E. 29th St., New York
(212) 683-4833 or 483-6833

The Comic Strip
1568 2nd Ave., New York
(212) 861-9386

Dangerfields
1118 First Ave., New York
(212) 593-1650

The First Amendment Comedy
  Cabaret
2 Bond St., New York
(212) 473-1472

The Improvisation
358 W. 44th St.
(212) 765-8268

Stand-up New York
236 W. 78th St., New York
(212) 595-0850

Banana Comedy Club
Holiday Inn, Rt. 9, Sharon Drive,
  Poughkeepsie
(914) 471-5002

Mr. M's
30 Winthrope Ln., Scarsdale

East End Comedy
91 Hill St., Southhampton
(516) 283-6500

Wise Guys
117 Bruce St., Syracuse
(315) 475-0866

North Carolina
Cabana Comedy Club
I-40 and High Point Rd.,
  Greensboro
(919) 294-4920

Charlie Goodnights
861 W. Morgan St., Raleigh
(919) 832-0998

Ohio
The Akron-Canton Comedy Club
5719 Fulton Rd., Canton

Cleveland Comedy Club
2230 E. 4th St., Cleveland
(216) 696-9266

■ 187

Hilarities Comedy Hall
1230 W. 6th St., Cleveland
(216) 781-7735

Hilarities
1546 State Rd., Cuyahoga Falls
(216) 923-4700

The Funny Bone Comedy Club
6312 Buesch Blvd., Columbus

Kelly's Komedy Klub
Dayton Ramada Inn South, Dayton

Wiley's Comedy Club
970 Patterson Rd., Dayton
(513) 294-4744

The Funny Bone Comedy Club
8140 Market Place, Montgomery
(513) 984-LAFF

Cartoons
37415 Euclid Ave., Willoughby

Oklahoma
Tulsa Comedy Club
5015 So. 78 East Ave., Tulsa
(918) 664-2523

Jokers Comedy Club
2920 W. Britton Rd., Oklahoma
 City
(405) 752-5270

Oregon
The Last Laugh
426 NW 6th Ave., Portland
(503) 29-LAUGH

Pennsylvania
Bucks County Comedy Cabaret
Atop Poco's, 625 N. Main St.,
 Doylestown
(215) 345-JOKE

King of Prussia Comedy Cabaret
George Washington Lodge, Rt.
 202S
Warner Rd., King of Prussia
(215) 265-2030

Media Comedy Stop
1124 W. Baltimore Pike, Media
(215) 891-7500

The Comedy Factory Outline
31 Bank St., Philadelphia
(215) FUNNY-11

The Comedy Works
126 Chestnut St., Philadelphia
(215) WACKY-97

South Carolina
The Punch Line
628 Harden St., Columbia
(803) 779-5233

The Punch Line
915 E. Stone Ave., Greenville
(803) 235-5233

The Comedy Cafe
5900 Rivers Ave., N. Charleston
(803) 554-4292

South Dakota
Noodles Comedy Club at the
 Spaghetti Works Restaurant
5th and Phillips, Sioux Falls
(605) 334-0043

Tennessee
The Comedy Station
Regency Center (1-81 & Hwy.
  11W), Bristol
(615) 968-9119

The Funny Bone Comedy Club
7213-A Kingston Pike, Knoxville
(615) 588-5155

Sir Lafs-A-Lot
535 S. Highland, Memphis
(901) 324-JOKE

Zanie's Comedy Showplace
2025 8th Ave., South, Nashville
(615) 269-0221

Texas
Jolly's
2511 Paramount A-5, Amarillo
(806) 359-3432

The Funny Bone Comedy Club
2525 E. Arkansas Ct., Arlington
(817) 265-2277

Laff Stop
8120 Research Blvd., Austin
(512) 467-2333

Comedy Corner
8202 Parklane, Dallas
(214) 361-7461

The Funny Bone Comedy Club
12101 Greenville Ave., Dallas

The Comic Strip in the Park at
  Alto Mesa
6633 N. Mesa, El Paso
(915) 581-8877

The Funny Bone Comedy Club

4744 Bryant Irving Rd., Fort
  Worth
(817) 292-5552

Comedy Showcase
12547 Gulf Freeway, Houston
(713) 481-1188

Comedy West
Hyatt Regency West, 13210 Katy
  Freeway, Houston
(713) 558-1234

The Laff Stop
1952-AW. Gray, Houston
(713) 524-2333

Comedy Workshop
2105 San Felipe, Houston
(713) 524-7333

A Good Humor Bar
4444 Fm 1960 W 1, Houston
(713) 444-4312

Spellbinders Comedy Club
10001 Westheimer, Houston

Comedy Cabaret
204 Bender Ave., Humble
(713) 540-1543

San Antonio Comedy Club
12731 1-8th West, San Antonio
(512) 692-3443

Utah
Cartoons
3125 Washington Blvd., Odgen
(801) 392-7456

Cartoons
2201 S. Highland, Salt Lake City
(801) 485-LAFF

Virginia
Blacksburg Comedy Club
900 Plantation Rd., Blacksburg
(703) 552-7770

Comedy Club at Matt's British Pub
109 S. 12th St., Shockoe Slip,
Richmond
(804) 644-0848

Roanoke Comedy Club/Down the
Hatch at the Patrick Henry Hotel
617 Jefferson Ave., Roanoke
(703) 982-5693

Comedy Club at the
Thoroughgood Inn
4520 Independence Blvd., Virginia
Beach
(804) 499-2500

Washington
The Comedy Penthouse at Bailey's
Eatery & Bar
821 Bellevue Way NE, Bellevue
(206) 455-4494

Thydolough's
515 George Washington Way,
Richland
(509) 946-4121

The Comedy Underground
222 S. Main, Seattle
(206) 622-9353

Giggles Comedy Nightclub
5220 Roosevelt Way NE, Seattle
(206) 526-JOKE

Shananigan's
3017 Ruston Way, Tacoma
(206) 752-8811

T.R. Garrity's
2306 California Ave. SW, Seattle
(206) 935-1828

The Comedy Underground at
Chicago Subway
N3 Post Rd., Spokane
(509) 624-4050

Washington, D.C.
Comedy Cafe
1520 "K" St., NW
(202) 638-JOKE

Garvin's Laugh-Inn
1054 31st NW Canal Square,
Georgetown
(202) 342-2026

West Virginia
Cheers
101 Capitol St., Charleston
(216) 932-2535

The Ritz
1203 Virginia East, Charleston
(304) 343-1050

Robby's
809 3rd Avenue, Huntington
(304) 522-9714

Wisconsin
The Funny Bone Comedy Club
1434 N. Farwell, Milwaukee
(414) 273-1330

Picadilly Comedy Club at the
Concourse Hotel
1 Dayton Ave., Madison
(608) 257-6000

About the Authors

RICHARD BELZER was born in Bridgeport, Connecticut, and thrown out of or asked politely to leave every school he ever attended "due to uncontrollable wit." Belzer has parlayed his talent outside the classroom into a career that has spanned two decades.

He kicked off his career in show business with a starring role in *Groove Tube,* the counterculture film that went on to become a cult classic. Since then, Belzer's comedic talents have been featured in every show business medium: off Broadway *(The National Lampoon Show);* radio (*The Brink and Belzer Morning Show* on WNBC); movies *(Fame, Author, Author, Night Shift, Scarface, The Wrong Guys,* and *Freeway);* television (appearances on *Saturday Night Live, The Tonight Show, Late Night with David Letterman,* as a regular on *Thicke Of The Night,* as host of the Lifetime cable show *Hot Properties,* and in his own six-part comedy series on Cinemax, *The Richard Belzer Show*); and nightclubs, regularly appearing around the country in such clubs as Caroline's, The Improv, and Catch a Rising Star.

Richard Belzer lives with his wife, actress Harlee McBride, and their two daughters, Jessica and Bree.

LARRY CHARLES is the author of the Bible and most of Shakespeare's plays. He possesses amazing telekinetic abilities and X-ray vision, but he has solemnly pledged to use them only for the good of humanity. Occasionally, however, he makes buildings crumble and then combs the wreckage for free office supplies. He is currently ghostwriting his own memoirs, entitled *Larry Charles: The Man, the Smell.*

RICK NEWMAN is the founder of the world-famous comedy club, Catch a Rising Star. His insights into comedy and comedians, gained firsthand from experience and observation, have cast him as a sponsor and patron to most of today's top comedians and as a pivotal influence in shaping today's exploding world of comedy. Today, as a television producer and personal manager, Rick is at the forefront in expanding and exploring new comedy for the nineties.